Tintin

Inquisitive reporter Tintin is always trying to get to the bottom of mysteries.
Even when things get really spooky he manages to keep a cool head.

Captain Haddock

Captain Haddock would do anything to rescue his friend Professor Calculus.
But it is when he unwittingly falls for a painful practical joke
that a vital clue to Calculus's whereabouts is revealed!

Snowy

Tintin's faithful friend Snowy is a pretty tough dog.
But even he can't keep calm for long when Bianca Castafiore bursts into song!

Professor Calculus

Tintin's friend Professor Calculus decides to try on a gold bracelet he finds while out on a walk, but little does he realise what he is letting himself in for.

Thomson and Thompson

Police detectives Thomson and Thompson have been assigned
as guards to Dr Midge of the Darwin Museum.
Unfortunately all it takes is a butterfly to distract them from their duty!

Professor Tarragon

An expert in ancient America and member of the Sanders-Hardiman
Ethnographic Expedition, Professor Tarragon also happens to be
an old friend of Professor Calculus.

General Alcazar

General Alcazar is in temporary exile from his home country of San Theodoros.
To make ends meet he works as a knife-thrower in a breathtaking stage act.

THE SEVEN CRYSTAL BALLS

HOME AFTER TWO YEARS

Sanders-Hardiman Expedition Returns

LIVERPOOL, *Thursday*. The seven members of the Sanders-Hardiman Ethnographic Expedition landed at Liverpool today. Back in Europe after a fruitful two-year trip through Peru and Bolivia, the scientists report that their travels took them deep into little-known territory. They discovered several Inca tombs, one of which contained a mummy still wearing a 'borla' or royal crown of solid gold. Funerary inscriptions establish beyond doubt that the tomb belonged to the Inca Rascar Capac.

This will lead to trouble . . . You see if it doesn't!

What'll lead to trouble?

All this mummy business. Remember, young man, what happened with Tut-Ankh-Amen!

Think of all those Egyptologists, dying in mysterious circumstances after they'd opened the tomb of the Pharaoh . . . You wait, the same will happen to those busy-bodies, violating the Inca's burial chamber.

You think so?

I'm sure of it! . . . Anyway, why can't they leave them in peace? . . . What'd we say if the Egyptians or the Peruvians came over here and started digging up our kings? . . . What'd we say then, eh?

Well, I . . .

Oh . . . excuse me. I see we're coming to my station . . . I must go.

MARLINSPIKE

WAY OUT

Here we are . . .

Good morning, Nestor. Is the Captain at home?

No, Mr Tintin, the master is out at the moment. He went riding . . .

But he won't be long now. Look . . . You see . . .

Here comes his horse . . .

!

And there's the master.

Hello, Captain! . . .

Good day, my dear sir, good day. Excuse me for just a moment . . .

Nestor! . . . Nestor! . . . Bring me another, please!

Coming, sir . . .

Thank you, Nestor.

'Pon my word, it's Tintin!
. . . Delighted to see you,
my dear chap!

What fair wind brings you here?

I just dropped in to say hello . . .
to you and Professor Calculus
. . . How   is he?

Oh, he's fine . . . Here he comes now
. . . Still crazy about his dowsing,
as you see . . . The dear fellow is
convinced that there's a Saxon
burial-ground in the neighbourhood,
so he's decided to find it.

Hello, Professor
Calculus.

Why, it's our good
friend Tintin! What a
delightful surprise!

You're staying with us
for some time, I hope?

I'm afraid not.
I have to go home
this evening.

Excellent!
Excellent! What
good news! Nothing
could please me more.

Well, I'll see you later . . . I must
get   on with my work . . .

Let's leave the old boy to his
treasure-hunt, while we have a drink.

Apropos of a drink . . .
I've just   remembered . . .

!

Come with me. I've got something
amazing to show you . . .

WOOAH!
WOOAH!

Wooah! . . . Wooah!

FFFFFH
WOOAH
GRR
SCHH

You see, you miserable animal! That's your handiwork!

Oh, don't bother about him. Come with me . . .

You're going to see something fantastic!

Here we are.

Now, my dear fellow, just keep your eyes open.

First, another monocle . . .

There . . . Now, watch . . . I begin by pouring plain water into this glass . . . Note that; nothing but plain water.

Now, pay attention . . . This is it. Watch me very closely. I'm going to begin.

You see this? I have here a hollow cardboard cylinder . . . Hollow, you understand. Look . . . There's nothing inside, is there?

No, it seems quite empty.

But what on earth did you expect it to be?

Whisky, by thunder! . . . Whisky!

Whisky? . . . Come now, Captain, you can't be serious. How in the world could water turn itself into whisky? . . . It's impossible!

Impossible! Impossible! . . . No, blistering barnacles, it's not impossible. He manages it every time!

Who's he?

Bruno, the master magician! He's appearing at the Hippodrome. I've studied his act for a solid fortnight, trying to discover how he does it . . .

Yesterday I thought I'd solved it at last. Blistering barnacles, what do I get? Water, water, and still more water! But I'm going back again tonight, and you're coming too! This time I'll get the answer!

You must watch carefully to see exactly what he does . . .

We've got plenty of time. There are several other turns before he comes on.

First we have Ragdalam the fakir, with Yamilah, the amazing clairvoyant. Then Ramon Zarate, the knife-thrower. Next . . .

Ssh! Here comes Ragdalam the fakir. He's incredible too.

Ladies and gentlemen, I have much pleasure in inviting you to participate in a remarkable experiment: an experiment I had the honour to conduct . . .

. . . before his Highness the Maharaja of Hambalapur, and for which he invested me with the Order of the Grand Naja . . . The secret of the mysterious power at my command was entrusted to me by the famous yogi, Chandra Patnagar Rabad . . . And now, ladies and gentlemen, it is my privilege to introduce to you one of the most amazing personalities of the twentieth century . . .

I present: Madame Yamilah!

First I will put Madame Yamilah into a hypnotic trance . . .

Madame Yamilah, are you ready to answer me?

Yes, master . . .

Good . . . Tell me, Madame Yamilah, what is this gentleman's Christian name?

Augustus.

Is that correct, sir?

Yes . . . quite correct!

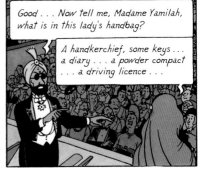

Good . . . Now tell me, Madame Yamilah, what is in this lady's handbag?

A handkerchief, some keys . . . a diary . . . a powder compact . . . a driving licence . . .

And the number on that licence, Madame Yamilah?

Seven six eight one three seven . . .

Absolutely right!

Fantastic, isn't it?

Madame Yamilah, will you please tell me whether that lady there in the third row is married.

Yes, she is married.

Good . . . And what is her husband's profession?

Photographer.

Is that right, madam?

Quite right.

I see him . . . returning from a long journey to a distant land . . . He . . . he . . . What is happening? . . . He is ill . . . very ill . . . with a mysterious sickness . . .

Look here, if this is a joke it's in very poor taste! . . . My husband is perfectly fit . . . This is absurd!

It is a deadly sickness . . . The vengeance of the Sun God is terrible indeed . . . His curse is upon him!

EEEEEK!

!

Ladies and gentlemen, we are interrupting the programme for a moment as we have an urgent message for a member of the audience . . . Will Mrs Clarkson, who is believed to be here tonight, please return home immediately, as her husband has just been taken seriously ill.

No, it's impossible! . . . It must be a put-up job!

I don't think so . . . Clarkson was the name of the photographer who accompanied the Sanders-Hardiman expedition.

Ladies and gentlemen, this unfortunate incident has so upset Madame Yamilah that we are going straight on to the next number . . . It is our pleasure to bring to you the world-famous knife-thrower, Ramon Zárate!

You'll see: he's a remarkable fellow.

Haven't I seen that face somewhere before? . . .

Señores and señoras, the performance I make for you is extremely peligroso . . . Por favor, I ask if you so kindly keep absoluto silencio . . .

May I borrow your glasses for a moment, Captain?

Great snakes! It's General Alcazar! . . .

General who?

Alcazar . . . You remember, he used to be President of the Republic of San Theodoros. I wonder what's landed him on the music-hall stage.

Now, is muy dificil!

Is more dificil!

Now, is mucho more dificil!

And now, señores and señoras, I perform for you, the first time done in Europe, the knife-throw with the eyes blindfold . . . Por favor, I ask someone come on to the stage to bandage for me the eyes.

There, that's it.

Muchas gracias, señor . . .

It almost went wrong three nights ago! The knife landed just on the edge of the target. Half an inch further and that Indian would have been skewered!

¿Esta usted?

¡si!

¡Muy bien!

Well, what do you think? Amazing, wasn't it?

Yes, it was very good.

Let's see what's coming next . . . Here we are . . . Good heavens!

Look, Bianca Castafiore, the Milanese nightingale!

Yes, I thought you'd be surprised!

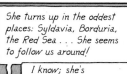

She turns up in the oddest places: Syldavia, Borduria, the Red Sea . . . She seems to follow us around!

I know; she's indefatigable! Here she comes! . . .

Ladies and gentlemen, tonight by special request I would like to sing for you the Jewel Song from "Faust".

Ah, my beauty past compare, These jewels bright I wear

MARGARITA EVER WAS!

Powerful stuff, eh?

You've said it!

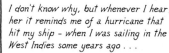

I don't know why, but whenever I hear her it reminds me of a hurricane that hit my ship – when I was sailing in the West Indies some years ago . . .

IS IT! IS IT!

Come reply! Mirror, mirror, tell me truly! Reply! Reply!

WOW-OW-WOOOW-OOOW

! !

WOOW-WOOOOW-OW-OW-OW-OOOW!

?

NO! NO! IT IS NOT!

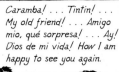
Caramba! . . . Tintin! . . . My old friend! . . . Amigo mio, qué sorpresa! . . . Ay! Dios de mi vida! How I am happy to see you again.

And this person here is what?

You remember, my friend Captain Haddock.

Los amigos de nuestros amigos son nuestros amigos! . . . I am happy Señor Colonel, so happy!

Delighted!

Descuida, no es la policia . . .

Ah! Bueno!

Poor Chiquito! . . . You understand . . . Ever since police come to look at our passports and our papers, he find police everywhere.

Yes, I quite see.

Por favor, we celebrate this happy meeting. You take with me a glass of aguardiente.

Your good health, amigo mio! Your good health, Señor Colonel!

Here's to you, General!

Good health!

Look out, it's awfully strong!

Strong? . . . Pooh! . . . I'm used to it, my dear fellow . . .

You are surprised to see me tonight on the music-hall stage, no? . . . That is life! . . . What can we do? There is another revolution in my country . . .

. . . and that mangy dog, General Tapioca, has seized power. So, I must leave San Theodoros. After I try many different jobs, I become a knife-thrower.

Sorry to interrupt, but it's time we were getting back to our seats; otherwise we'll miss the conjuror.

Yes, you're right.

I'm very sorry we have to leave you so soon. You see, we rather want to watch the conjuror do his act . . . Goodbye, General.

Adios, amigo mio.

Quick, or we shall miss the turn!

Still, I mustn't let it get me down.

Help! Help!

Captain!

Stop, Captain, stop!

... And what have we here in this glass, ladies and gentlemen? Water? No, this glass contains whisky! Yes, whisky, ladies and gentlemen . . . and if someone from the audience will be so kind as to step on to the stage . . .

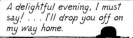
A delightful evening, I must say! . . . I'll drop you off on my way home.

Two days later . . .

MYSTERY ILLNESS STRIKES AGAIN

First Clarkson, now Sanders-Hardiman

Late last night Mr. Peter Clarkson, 37, photographer to the Sanders-Hardiman expedition to South America, was suddenly taken ill at his home. A few hours later Professor Sanders-Hardiman was found in a co . . . bedroom.

Think of all those Egyptologists, dying in mysterious circumstances after they'd opened the tomb of the Pharaoh . . . You wait, the same will happen to those busy-bodies, violating the Inca's burial chamber.

There could be something in what that chap said . . . Who knows? . . . I wonder . . .

RRRING

Hello! . . . How are things?

Hmm . . . All right . . . Yes, all right . . . We can't deny that we're right as ever.

Quite right . . . quite right . . . To be precise: we can deny that we're ever right.

Just as usual, eh?

Er . . . quite . . . You've seen this morning's paper? . . . "Mystery illness strikes again"? . . . Professor Sanders-Hardiman?

Yes, I saw that.

Good . . . Well . . . What's your view of this business?

I don't know. It certainly seems rather odd to me; but still, it could be pure coincidence.

No, no, there's more to it than just coincidence . . .

You're probably right, but how can you prove it? . . . Anyway, what is this mysterious illness? . . . What is it like?

Strictly speaking, it isn't exactly an illness . . . The two victims were found asleep: one at his desk, the other in his library. According to a preliminary report, the explorers seem to have fallen into some sort of deep coma or hypnotic sleep . . .

Oh? How very strange . . .

But have a look here . . .

?

Well? . . . They're little pieces of glass.

Pieces of crystal . . . they were found close to the two victims.

Have you thought of having these crystal fragments analysed?

Yes, I've left some of them at the laboratory at police headquarters. They're working on them now.

There it is: that's all we know so far.

Anyway, it's enough for us to rule out the theory of simple coincidence . . . What we need now is the result of the police analysis. I wonder . . .

I'll ring up the laboratory. Perhaps they've got the answer already.

Good.

Hello? . . . Headquarters? . . . Put me through to the laboratory, please . . . Hello, Doctor Simons? . . . This is Thomson . . . No, without a P, as in Venezuela . . . Yes . . . the analysis . . . Well?

What??

Professor Reedbuck! . . . It's fantastic! . . . Found asleep in his bath . . . Yes . . . They discovered the same crystal fragments . . . Incredible! . . . I say, how is the analysis getting on? . . . Have you . . . ?

Nothing definite yet . . . We've established that the glass particles come from little crystal balls . . . These probably contained the substance . . .

. . . which sent the unfortunate victims into a sort of coma . . . The substance? We have absolutely no idea . . . Yes, we're pressing on with our tests . . . I'll let you know how things are going. Goodbye.

I can't believe it! Professor Bathtub, found asleep in the reeds!

Number three!

We must warn the other members of the expedition at once! And we must get police protection for them.

Why? . . . You don't think that they . . . that we . . . that it . . . ?

Of course! There's no reason why this should stop. Everyone who took part in the expedition is in danger. Let's see . . . Sanders-Hardiman, Clarkson, Reedbuck: that's three . . . Who were the others? . . . Oh yes! Mark Falconer. Ring up Mark Falconer.

Hello? . . . Hello? . . . Hello? . . . Hello?

It's always the same with the telephone: whenever you need it, it's guaranteed to be out of order!

There's no reply?

I hate to interfere, but if I were you I'd try using that.

Is that Mark Falconer?

Yes, Falconer speaking . . .

Yes . . . yes . . . yes, I was just reading the paper . . . What? Professor Reedbuck too? . . . And . . . no . . . What's that? Crystal fragments! . . . By Jupiter, so he was telling the truth!

Who? . . . An old Indian, who got drunk on coca one night. He told me . . . No, I can't explain over the telephone . . . No, I'll come along and see you . . . Where? . . . Good!

I'll pick up a taxi and be with you right away. Meanwhile, warn Cantonneau, Midge and Tarragon. Tell them to stay indoors. And above all to keep away from the windows . . . Yes, windows . . . Me? Don't worry, I shall be on my guard . . . Goodbye for now. I'll be with you soon.

He's coming here. He seemed to know all about it . . . He said we should warn the other explorers, telling them not to go out, and to keep away from the windows.

Good, I'll warn Professor Cantonneau . . .

Something's happened to Professor Cantonneau! . . . I'm going straight round there . . . You stay here and warn the other two explorers at once.

There's a taxi pulling up outside the door.

I expect it's brought Mr Falconer . . . I'll take it on.

Hurry, Snowy! Hurry!

Here we are, sir: sixty-five pence . . .

?

!

The same crystal fragments!

Your passenger – he's been attacked! Tell me, did you stop anywhere on the way?

No . . . oh, yes. Once, at a junction, when the lights were against me.

Now I remember! It must have happened then . . . Another taxi drew up alongside mine, and I heard a faint sound of glass breaking. I didn't think much of it at the time. The lights changed, and we moved off.

I see. Go into the house and up to the first floor, where you'll find two police officers. Tell them your story. I'm off to warn Doctor Midge.

Righto!

21

... of the seven explorers who took part in the expedition, only Doctor Midge and Professor Tarragon have escaped the fate of their colleagues. A day-and-night police watch is being kept on their homes, and on the office of Doctor Midge, Director of the Darwin Museum ...

DARWIN MUSEUM

Halt, or I fire! ...

I've got to deliver a registered letter and a parcel to Doctor Midge ...

All right. Go on in.

Thank you, sir.

Aha! How splendid! One of my colleagues in Java has sent me an unknown species of butterfly he caught out there.

Most exciting! Now, let's see this strange lepidopter ...

Stop! Don't open that parcel! It may be a booby-trap! ... Give it to me: I will open it myself.

But what about you ... ?

It is my duty, Dr Midge, my duty ... To be precise: headquarters expects that every detective will do his duty.

I say, come on in, quickly. There's a suspicious parcel to be looked into.

Here's the p-p-parcel.

We'd b-b-better open it . . . Keep c-c-calm!

That's right: keep c-c-calm!

C-c-careful! . . .

C-c-careful! . . .

DIRECTOR

Whew! It's all right: false alarm . . . It's just a butterfly . . . And what a butterfly! . . . Look . . .

It's magnificent!

Between ourselves, let's face it – that was a narrow escape . . .

Between ourselves, to be precise: I agree!

DIREC

Ssh! Someone's coming . . .

DIREC

Hello, all well?

DIRECTOR

Ah, it's Tintin.

Yes, all's well. But we had a narrow escape. We've just opened a parcel which looked rather suspicious. Luckily, it was only a butterfly. Look, here it is . . .

What a beauty!

ECTOR

Good. I see Dr Midge's door is well guarded. What about his window?

His window? I'm guarding that. What more need I say?

TOR

You're guarding his window? Then what are you doing in here?

Great Scotland Yard, I . . .

ECTO

ZZING
CLING
CLING

DIRECTOR

Goodness gracious!
He's asleep too!

ZZZZ
ZZZZ

?

Over there! Someone's
just disappeared into
the shrubbery!

Hello, Headquarters? . . . This is Thompson . . .
Yes, with a P, as in Philadelphia . . . Yes . . .
I'm very well, thank you . . . It's Dr Midge who
isn't . . . I mean . . . Yes, sir . . . They've got
him too.

That way, Snowy! . . .
Hurry! . . . Hurry!

After him, Snowy!
. . . Catch him!

CRACK

Wooah!
Wooah!

All right, Snowy!
. . . Hang on!
. . . I'm coming!

WOOAH

CRACK

Here I come! . . .
Don't let him go! . . .

?

Wooah!
Wooah!

A cat! All that fuss for a
miserable cat! Meanwhile, of
course, our quarry has got
clean away . . . . Come on
now, get going!

The next morning...

Daily Reporter

MYSTERY OF THE CRYSTAL BALLS

Director of Darwin Museum is new victim

DR. MIDGE IN COMA

Was it done? How ... | Tarts | Doctor Midge | Pol

Extraordinary! . . . Quite extraordinary! . . . Another victim . . . It's amazing!

No, I think it's a little to the left.

No, I said: another victim. Here in the newspaper . . . The Director of the Darwin Museum . . . Doctor Midge.

Not yet, but I'm sure to get there in the end.

Yes. Good. There. Read it yourself . . . It's simpler that way . . .

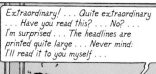

Extraordinary! . . . Quite extraordinary . . . Have you read this? . . . No? . . . I'm surprised . . . The headlines are printed quite large . . . Never mind: I'll read it to you myself . . .

"The Mystery of the Crystal Balls, as it is now generally known, continues to hit the front page. Is this the vengeance of a fanatical Indian? Has he sworn to punish those who were bold enough to disturb the tomb of the Inca king, Rascar Capac? All the evidence . . .

. . . points that way, and this dramatic theory cannot be discounted. But it poses new questions. Why did the mysterious avenger not kill his victims on the spot? Why, instead, plunge them into a profound sleep? . . .

RRRING

. . . a sleep which, says medical opinion, could be prolonged for an indefinite period without imperilling their lives. Readers are already familiar with the details of the . . ."

Good morning, Nestor. Is the Captain at home?

Yes, sir . . . Come in.

Wooah! Wooah!

Pffft!

Tintin, my dear fellow!
... How very nice!

How are you? And how's Professor Calculus?

Very well. He's busy reading the paper to me ...

" ... The police are taking full precautions to ensure the safety of the last of the seven members of the expedition. This move is welcome. It is certain ...

... that otherwise he would swiftly share the fate of his colleagues. Today, Professor Tarragon ..." Oh!

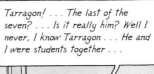
Tarragon! ... The last of the seven? ... Is it really him? Well I never, I know Tarragon ... He and I were students together ...

You know Professor Tarragon, the expert on ancient America? ... Isn't he the one with the Rascar Capac mummy in his possession?

Oh, no! On the contrary,. he's most kind ... I'll introduce you to him if you like.

I'd enjoy meeting him. Thank you.

You'd like to go now? ... Certainly ... Come along ...

Look, visitors for Professor Tarragon.

We'd like to see Professor Tarragon ...

Have you a pass?

Haddock, Tintin and Calculus ... Right. Wait here, and I'll see if you can go in.

It's like trying to get into a fortress!

We have our orders ...

OK, these gentlemen can come in.

HA - HA - HA - HA - HA!

Here's the culprit . . . Our friend Rascar Capac frightened your dog . . . Rascar Capac: he-who-unleashes-the-fire-of-heaven.

BOOM

What about that! We were just talking about Rascar Capac, he-who-unleashes-the-fire-of-heaven, and I think he's going to oblige: look . . .

You have an open car, I believe . . . If I were you, I'd put it under cover right away. These summer storms can be very violent . . . an absolute downpour . . .

Thanks. May I put it in the garage?

Did you hear that? . . . Sounded like a shot outside . . .

BANG

Over there . . . a man running . . . It's one of the detectives guarding the house . . .

Quick, let's see what's happening . . .

That came from the direction of the gates.

BANG

28

Everything all right? . . . Good, good . . . At any rate, the false alarm did prove that the house is well guarded.

Yes, it certainly seems to be. But still, we must be very careful.

By the way, Professor, what do you make of this whole business of the crystal balls?

What do I make of it? . . . Not much . . . But, as a matter of fact, I've drafted a paper . . .

. . . on the occult practices of ancient Peru. It seems to have some bearing, but I doubt if it will solve our problem.

Look at this . . . it's a translation of part of the inscriptions carved on the walls of Rascar Capac's tomb . . . You may like to read it.

"After many moons will come seven strangers with pale faces; they will profane the sacred dwellings of he-who-unleashes-the-fire-of-heaven. These vandals will carry the body of the Inca to their own far country. But the curse of the gods will be as their shadow and pursue them over land and sea . . ."

But . . . but . . . this is quite extraordinary!

Isn't it? . . . But read the next bit . . .

CRACK

Rascar Capac's disappeared! ... Vaporized! ... Vanished into thin air! ... There's nothing left but the jewels!

But Professor Tarragon ... what's the matter?

I ... it's nothing ... Read the rest ... the rest of my translation.

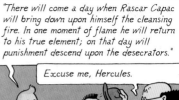

"There will come a day when Rascar Capac will bring down upon himself the cleansing fire. In one moment of flame he will return to his true element; on that day will punishment descend upon the desecrators."

Excuse me, Hercules.

The prophecy is fulfilled ... Rascar Capac has gone ... and I am struck down by his curse ... I feel it! ...

Me too! ... And it smells very strong: sulphur, isn't it?

Don't give in! The house is well guarded; you know that. Where do you sleep?

In the next room. There are no windows.

Good. And there are shutters in here ... What's more, we are upstairs. To make doubly sure, we'll station two policemen outside these windows ... You see, there's absolutely no danger.

You're right ... I'm being absurd ... Let me show you to your rooms, then I'll bid you good-night.

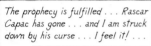

Some hours later ...

ZING

⟨32⟩

Whew! What a relief . . . It was only a dream . . . The gale blew the window open!

Still, it was a horrible nightmare!

HELP! . . . HELP!

That's the Captain's voice!

THUMP

What's happened, Captain? . . . I thought I heard you shouting.

Yes, I . . . I had a frightful nightmare! . . . Rascar Capac came into my room . . . He had a huge crystal ball in his hand . . . he hurled it down on the floor . . .

Incredible! . . . The same dream as mine!

OOH OOH

Now what is it?

Look out! . . . He's there! . . . He's after me! . . . He's coming! . . .

But it's impossible . . . every single exit is guarded . . .

Professor Tarragon! Professor Tarragon!

There's nothing we can do . . . The crystal ball has done its work . . . and claimed the last of the seven.

ZZZZZ . . . ZZZZ . . .

Quick, the window! . . . The intruder must have gone that way!

But no . . . the window and the shutter are closed tight . . . it's incredible!

Has anyone gone past you?

No, sir, no one at all . . . Why?

This absolutely beats me . . . How did the fellow make his getaway?

Oh! Look over there! Rascar Capac's jewels have disappeared!

WOOAH! WOOAH!

There! That's how it was done . . . the attacker came and went by the chimney!

Wooah! Wooah!

Well, if he went up here, there's still time - he can't have got clean away . . .

?

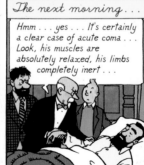

Well, well, well . . . What have we here?

A bracelet! . . . Well I never! It's the one that was on the mummy! . . . How very curious . . . How did it come to be here?

Magnificent! . . . It's obviously made of solid gold . . . I'll put it on and go indoors wearing it, and see if they notice . . .

Really splendid . . . And how well it goes with my coat!

A few minutes later . . .

Calculus? . . . Out in the garden . . . I expect he's hard at work with his pendulum. Wait; I'll go and find him.

Now where's old Cuthbert got to?

Strange, I'm sure he said he was going into the garden.

Hello . . . Did you find him?

No, he wasn't there. He's probably back in his room . . . I'll go up and look . . .

No, he's not in his room. That's rather odd . . .

Let's go back into the garden. I expect we'll find him in the shrubbery with that beloved pendulum of his.

CALCULUS!
CALCULUS!

It's no good shouting for *him!*

Now where's the old goat hidden himself? . . . Calculus!!!

CALCULUS!

?

Captain! . . . Captain! Look up there!

Bloodstains! The imprint of a hand! . . . What does that mean? Who could have . . .

Who? . . . The intruder last night, I'll bet . . . No wonder we couldn't find him . . . Wounded, and chased like that, he didn't know which way to turn . . . so he took refuge in the top of this tree . . .

But . . . he could still be up there . . .

You're right . . . I'm going to see for myself . . .

Do be careful . . . Take my gun with you.

Good idea. Thanks . . .

Any luck?

No, I still can't see anything . . .

CRACK

I'm all right, Captain . . . only a rotten branch breaking . . .

You're all right, eh? What about me?

There's no one here now. I'm coming down.

Captain! . . . Over there, to your right, look! . . . More to the right . . . more . . . There, you've got it!

It's Calculus's umbrella!

It is his, isn't it?

Yes, of course it is! How in the . . .

Look there . . . The grass is all trampled down.

And these broken branches . . . There's been a fight here!

A fight? . . . Old Calculus been fighting?

Maybe not . . . But he's certainly been attacked . . . Now I see what happened . . . The intruder was still up in the tree . . . Along came Calculus . . . and the other fellow jumped on him.

But, blistering barnacles, why? Why on earth should anyone attack Calculus?

I don't know, Captain, I don't know. All I do know is that Professor Calculus has disappeared, and we've got to find him.

SNOWY! SNOWY! SNOWY!

Snowy! Snowy! Snowy!

You can have your bone back in a minute, Snowy. But first of all you must try to find the Professor.

Seek, Snowy, seek him out! . . . Go on . . . Quickly!

Is he in there?

Look out, Captain! . . . Look out! Take cover!

Why? . . . What is it?

Take cover!

BANG BANG

Tribe of savages! . . . Vampires! . . . Monsters!

Here, Captain . . . I've got the car number . . . We're not beaten yet . . . Come on, quickly! . . .

The inspector will pass the number on to his headquarters at once . . .

The rats!

Hello, Headquarters? This is Chambers . . . Yes . . . One of Professor Tarragon's friends has been kidnapped . . . Professor Cuthbert Calculus . . . Yes, in a car . . . I'll give you its number and a description . . .

An Opel.

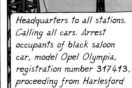

Headquarters to all stations. Calling all cars. Arrest occupants of black saloon car, model Opel Olympia, registration number 317413, proceeding from Harlesford in a south-westerly direction.

The brutes! . . . Kidnapping Calculus! . . . And why, may I ask? . . . What possible reason can they have for kidnapping poor Cuthbert?

RRRING RRRING

Hello? . . . Yes . . . Chambers speaking . . . Oh, yes sir . . . Right . . . right . . . you'll keep in touch? . . . Good!

Well, that's that . . . There are police check-points on all the roads in this area . . . they won't escape us . . . Never fear . . .

Diabolo! . . . The police!

PAAAARP

The swine!

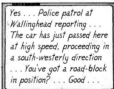

Yes . . . Police patrol at Wallinghead reporting . . . The car has just passed here at high speed, proceeding in a south-westerly direction . . . You've got a road-block in position? . . . Good . . .

It beats me! . . . Which way did they go? . . . Ah, a workman. I'll have a word with him.

A black car? . . . I don't know if it's the one you're looking for, but a car turned down there about three-quarters of an hour ago . . . to the right, into the wood.

Good. Thanks.

!

RRRING RRRING

Hello, yes . . . yes . . . Well? . . . You've found it? That's splen . . . What? . . . Empty!

Quick, Captain, we'll hop in the car . . . We might learn something over there . . .

Nest of rattlesnakes! . . . Pirates! . . . Bashi-bazouks!

You found it here? Abandoned, like this?

Yes. But the occupants won't get far. The whole area is cordoned off, and we're beating the wood . . . The man they've kidnapped - is he a friend of yours?

It's Calculus, you poor loon! . . . Calculus! . . . The salt of the earth . . . with a heart of gold! He's been kidnapped by those devils! . . . Why? I ask you . . . Thundering typhoons, d'you know why?

Me? . . . No.

Well, Sherlock Holmes . . . Have you found anything?

Could be . . .

I say, officer, you were at one of the road-blocks weren't you? So you should have seen a large fawn-coloured car go by . . .

A large fawn car? Just let me think . . .

Good heavens, you're right! A fawn car did pass us . . . A saloon . . . I stopped it myself.

You didn't think of taking the number?

No . . . why should I? . . . But wait a bit . . . The driver looked like a foreigner: Spanish, or South American, or something like that . . . Fattish, sun-tanned, black moustache and side-boards, horn-rimmed glasses . . .

And the others? . . . There were some others, I suppose?

Yes, there was someone sitting beside him . . . Another foreigner, I'd say: dark hair, bony face, hooked nose, thin lips . . . I think there were two other men in the back, but I only caught a glimpse of them.

Good! . . . Well, you can call off the beaters . . . It's a waste of time. The kidnappers are far away.

Oh, yes? How do you know that?

How do I know? . . . Look at these tracks . . . Here are the tyre-marks of the Opel. But here are some others, different tyres. Dunlop I'd say: the tyres of the car that was waiting for the Opel.

Blistering barnacles, you're right! But how did you guess that it was fawn-coloured?

Look here . . .

Specks of fawn paint . . . The lane is narrow. In turning, one of the wings of the car scraped against this tree, leaving traces of paint.

The crooks! So they switched cars!

Come on, we must pass all this on to the police at once. Perhaps they'll be able to catch them further on . . .

The next morning . . .

Let's see . . . Ah, here . . .

"The car used by the kidnappers is a large fawn saloon . . ." Good . . . "The occupants are believed to be of South American origin . . ." That's right . . . "Anyone who can give any information is asked to get in touch with the nearest police station immediately."

Oh well, there's still some hope left . . .

RRRING
RRRING

Hello, this is Thomson . . . Yes, without a P . . . I say, there's something very queer going on at the hospital where the seven explorers are detained . . . I think you'd better slip round there . . .

It's really serious? . . . I can't believe it! . . . What? . . . Yes . . . Of course . . . Don't worry, I'll go round at once.

Yes, it is most extraordinary. Every day, at the same time, the seven patients go into some sort of trance . . . It's quite inexplicable . . . Look, it's almost time for their seizure now . . . You'll see what I mean . . .

Some of the leading consultants in this field are in the ward now, waiting for the symptoms to appear.

Here are the patients. You'll see . . .

They all look quite peaceful to me.

For the time being. But wait, it'll soon begin . . . There!

49

HOSPITAL

It's certainly very peculiar.

But what possible connection can there be between all this and the kidnapping of Calculus?

The next day . . .

Good afternoon, Nestor. How is the Captain?

Oh sir, he's aged ten years since this trouble began . . . And you, sir? Have you any news?

None Nestor. Poor Professor Calculus has vanished into thin air.

Oh dear, oh dear! The master will be so disappointed.

He's there, sir.

Hello, Captain.

Ah, Tintin! Hello . . . Well, what about Calculus? Anything new?

Nothing at all, I'm afraid.

Thundering typhoons.

WOOAH GRRR FFFH

Snowy! . . . Here, Snowy!

Wooah! Wooah!

RRRRING

Hello . . . Yes, it's me . . . Who's that? . . . Oh? . . . Well, what news? . . . What?!

Meanwhile . . .

Just one more tot . . . the last . . .

My poor, poor friend. What has become of you?

Here's to you, Cuthbert old chap. We'll find you, I promise – dead or alive.

As I've told you before – more to the west!

And now perhaps you'll be kind enough to behave yourself. Otherwise it's a muzzle and lead . . . understand?

What is it now? Oh, you're thirsty? All right, go on.

Mm-m-m-m! This is what I call water!

A few minutes later...

And now, Captain, will you please tell me where we're going?

To Westermouth.

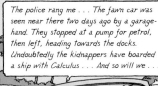

The police rang me... The fawn car was seen near there two days ago by a garage-hand. They stopped at a pump for petrol, then left, heading towards the docks. Undoubtedly the kidnappers have boarded a ship with Calculus... And so will we...

...by thunder, and snatch him from the grasp of those iconoclasts, those vampires, those... And just think: Westermouth, docks, jetties, the ocean, the sea-breezes whipping the spray in your face...

As for the spray, Captain, you've got your wish!

Blistering barnacles!... Quick, the hood, or we'll be drenched!

What's up?

Thundering typhoons, it's stuck!... Something's caught up... I'll try to do it from inside the car...

Billions of blistering barnacles!

That's got it!

About time too!

54

Thundering typhoons! I'm soaked!

Everything happens to me!

Oh, well, at least I'm a bit drier now . . .

Gangsters! . . . Road-hogs! . . . Mountebanks! Steamrollers! . . . Nyctalops! . . . Parasites!

Sea-gherkins! . . . Pock-marks! Cannibals!

Come on, Captain; hurry up, or we'll never get there.

As soon as we get to Westermouth tomorrow, we'll go straight to the police; they'll put us in the picture . . .

Early next morning . . .

I'm sorry, there's nothing fresh . . . It was a fawn car all right; but was it the one containing your friend? It was seen heading for Westermouth . . . and since then, nothing . . . it has simply vanished.

The search is continuing, that's all I can tell you. But in my opinion, there's very little chance . . . Excuse me . . .

Hello? . . . Yes, this is Inspector Jackson . . . Yes . . . Again? . . . What? . . . Where? . . . In one of the docks? . . . Well I'm . . . !! There's no mistake about it? . . . Excellent!

Well, gentlemen, you're in luck! The fawn car has just been recovered from one of the docks. If you'd like to come with me, we'll go and have a look.

Thanks very much!

It was a trawler, coming in. She struck an obstacle, so we dragged the dock . . . And there you are.

Is there any means of identification? . . . Number plate? . . . Licence? . . . Engine number?

Nothing at all, sir. There are no number plates, and the engine and chassis numbers have been filed off. It's a mass-produced car, so there isn't much chance of ever finding out . . .

Yes, I see . . .

Anyway, we can be certain of one thing: whoever kidnapped Professor Calculus embarked here, having first tried to get rid of the car by dumping it in the dock.

Yes . . . yes . . . perhaps . . .

We must act at once: we'll radio a description of your friend to all the ships that have sailed from Westermouth since the twelfth . . . Then we'll see what happens.

Thanks, Inspector – and you'll let us know how things are going?

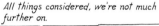

All things considered, we're not much further on.

I know.

Hello, she's leaving for South America . . . and the kidnappers could be aboard . . . with poor Calculus!

Great snakes! . . . That looks like . . . Yes, it is!

Hey! . . . Who are you?

Police!

Hello, General!

Ay Dios de mi vida!... Tintin! Amigo mio!

Nice to see you, General. Are you off on tour?

On tour?... Caramba!... I go home to my own country. Music-hall, for me is finished... No more partner.

No partner?... What's happened to Chiquito?

Gone!... Disappeared!... Four days ago... I not blame him... Before we come to Europe he say he leave me one day: not to worry, not to look for him... And, it is so.

Four days ago?... Then he disappeared on the twelfth... well, well. Tell me: is Chiquito a real Indian?

Is Chiquito a real Indian? Santa Madre de Dios!... He is one of last descendants of los Incas!

What? A descendant of the Incas?... You're sure of that?

Absolutely sure! He is pure-blooded Quichua Indian... Chiquito is just stage name. His real name is Rupac Inca Huaco.

Rupac Inca Huaco?... I wonder... The thin man beside the driver, in the fawn car...

The fawn car?

Have you ever seen Chiquito with a rather fat man with a small black moustache and horn-rimmed glasses?... Perhaps a Peruvian...

Never. He never see anybody, never speak to anybody except me...

TOOOOOT

Caramba! I must go now... Adios, amigo mio... We meet again, perhaps!

Good luck!

All aboard!

Well, who did you see over there?

General Alcazar.

He told me two very odd things... First his partner Chiquito disappeared on the twelfth... That was the night Professor Tarragon was attacked, and the mummy's jewels stolen. The next day Calculus was kidnapped.

Secondly, Chiquito's real name is Rupac Inca Huaco, and he's a descendant of the Incas!

What?

Strange coincidences, eh? Very strange... What do you say to that?

Hey!... Whoa!... Stop!...

?

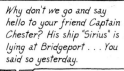
Why don't we go and say hello to your friend Captain Chester? His ship "Sirius" is lying at Bridgeport... You said so yesterday.

Good for you! Let's go...

Now where's the "Sirius"? Chester told me he was berthed at Quay No. 18... We'll have to ask someone...

The "Sirius"?... Yes, she was here... She sailed on this morning's tide... That's hard luck!

Hard luck! It certainly is!... If only we had some news of Calculus... the smallest clue...

Hard luck!

Yeoww!

It's the classic joke!... A stone hidden under an old hat!

Oww! Yoww!! Yeeoww!!!

There, Captain, look! Those boys... they did it!

Vagabonds!... Hooligans!... Iconoclasts!...

Captain! Captain! Don't do that! It's terribly dangerous!

Yes, you're right... Anyway, they're well out of range!

Still, if I get my hands on the young jackanapes they won't forget Captain Haddock in a hurry!

THUD *
?
SPLOSH

Whew, that was a near thing!

Hello, Snowy. What have you got there? . . . A hat?

Goodness, it's the same one . . . The one the Captain kicked.

There . . . And leave the dirty thing alone!

Here, Snowy! Come here! And put that hat down!

Why can't you do as you're told?

We'll put a stop to your little game . . .

Now! . . . At least you won't go in there after it!

?

Come along, Snowy! . . . Here!

Wooah! Wooah!

SPLASH

!

!

Oh, so you're trying to make a fool of me, are you?

Donkey! What do you want me to do with that hat? Wear it?

Then I'd look like . . . Crumbs! . . . No, it's impossible!

!

60

Captain! . . . Captain! . . . I've got Calculus's hat!

Old Cuthbert's little round hat! . . . That's why Snowy insisted on retrieving it . . . Look at the initials!

C.C.: Cuthbert Calculus! . . . But then . . .

Calculus wasn't taken aboard at Westermouth. It was here at Bridgeport . . . But what ship? . . . And what was her destination? . . . That's what we need to know.

But how can we find out?

I've got it! We must try to find those two lads who played the trick with the hat.

Yes! I'll teach the young pirates a thing or two!

On the contrary, Captain, you'll be very nice to them . . . After all, thanks to them we found the hat . . . and we want them to tell us how they came by it themselves.

Oh, yes . . .

Good old Snowy; because of you we've made a wonderful discovery . . . Now we want you to help us again . . . We must find those two scamps . . . you ran after them remember?

An hour later . . .

?

Hey, what's bitten you?

Hello there!

!

Don't worry, we're not looking for trouble. We just want to know where you found this hat?

That hat? . . . We were down in No. 17 shed this morning . . . where the crates were stacked for loading aboard . . .

. . . the "Black Cat" . . . When they lifted one of the crates out of the shed, I saw the hat underneath, all flattened out . . . Honestly, it wasn't my idea to play that trick . . . it was my friend . . .

Well, your friend had a jolly good idea . . . Didn't he, Captain?

Now, Captain, to the harbour master's office. We'll ask them when the packing-cases came into the warehouse.

The cases? . . . They arrived on the fourteenth, by rail . . . This morning they were loaded aboard the "Black Cat".

And the night before they arrived, was a ship berthed opposite shed No. 17?

On the thirteenth? . . . Let's see . . . Yes, the "Pachacamac" - a Peruvian merchantman. She arrived from Callao on the tenth with a cargo of guano; she sailed again for Callao on the fourteenth with a load of timber.

Fine. I'm most grateful to you.

As I see it, Calculus was kidnapped by Chiquito, a Peruvian Indian; he's aboard the "Pachacamac", a Peruvian ship, bound for a Peruvian port!

But, thundering typhoons, we must go after those gangsters at once! We must rescue him!

Agreed! We'll leave for Peru as soon as we can . . . Tomorrow, or the day after. Now I'm going to ring up the Inspector and tell him what we've discovered.

Good. And I'll telephone Nestor to tell him we're leaving.

Hello . . . yes, speaking . . . What? The Professor's hat? . . . You . . . Oh! . . . Yes . . . Of course . . . The "Pachacamac" . . . for Callao . . . It seems a very strong lead . . . Yes, I'll make the necessary arrangements . . . What? You're going to Callao? But that's absurd! . . . As you like . . . When are you leaving? . . . Right . . . Goodbye, and good luck!

The next day . . .

Excuse me, but that isn't the plane for South America taking off, is it?

Yes, that's her.

Oh dear! Oh dear! What a calamity! What a terrible calamity . . . The master! My poor, poor master!

What's up? Anything serious?

It is indeed! The master has left without a single spare monocle!

!

Now off to Peru! . . . We shall be in Callao well before the "Pachacamac". We'll get in touch with the police there at once, and as soon as the ship arrives, we'll rescue Calculus.

Yes, that's all very fine, but I wonder if it will be as easy as you think . . .

What will happen in Peru? You will find out in **PRISONERS OF THE SUN**

THE REAL-LIFE INSPIRATION
BEHIND
TINTIN'S ADVENTURES

Written by Stuart Tett
with the collaboration of Studio Moulinsart.

Discover something new and exciting

HERGÉ

© Studios Hergé

Victory

In September 1944, World War II was nearly over and Belgium was liberated of Nazi occupation by the Allied forces. A few months later Hergé sent four signed and decorated Tintin books to the son of a British army captain. The theme was victory! Check out the spitfire fighter plane – the pride of the British airforce – that Hergé drew in one of the books.

2

about Tintin and his creator Hergé!

TINTIN

His own magazine

An important thing happened while *The Seven Crystal Balls* was being written: together with an entrepreneur named Raymond Leblanc, Hergé launched a Belgian children's magazine titled *Tintin*!

At the time the stories we know today as *The Seven Crystal Balls* and its sequel *Prisoners of the Sun*, were one long story published in *Tintin* magazine as *Le Temple du Soleil*.

Promotional poster for *Tintin* magazine, 1946. The motto reads "The magazine for young people from 7-77 years old!"

THE TRUE STORY
...behind *The Seven Crystal Balls*

From the outset, *The Seven Crystal Balls* is a Tintin story with a terrifying twist. While on an ordinary train journey to see his friends at Marlinspike Hall, Tintin reads about the return of an expedition from ancient Inca territory in South America. Suddenly a fellow passenger pipes up with an ominous warning for the hapless explorers.

Think of all those Egyptologists, dying in mysterious circumstances after they'd opened the tomb of the Pharaoh... You wait, the same will happen to those busybodies, violating the Inca's burial chamber.

You think so?

There could be something in what that chap said... Who knows? ... I wonder...

For the rest of the adventure we are gripped – it's difficult not to be scared when all the supernatural stuff seems so real! So over the pages that follow you have to ask yourself, "Is this real or not?"

Once upon a time…

In the Young Readers edition of *Cigars of the Pharaoh* you can read about the discovery of the tomb of Tutankhamun (1922) and about one or two of the eerie misfortunes that befell some members of the team that discovered it. Although the leader, Howard Carter, was not personally struck down by a nasty surprise, he did record in his diary a "strange" incident when he saw jackals reminding him of Anubis, the Ancient Egyptian jackal-headed god and protector of tombs.

Tintin discovers a statue of Anubis –
and Dr Sarcophagus's tailcoat and cuffs! –
in the black and white version of
Cigars of the Pharaoh, 1934.

Monocled magician

When Tintin arrives at Marlinspike Hall, he is surprised to find Captain Haddock wearing a monocle and speaking with a funny accent. The Captain also has a surprise for Tintin – a magic trick! Hergé practised sketching his assistant Edgar Jacobs to catch the right pose.

It looks like Haddock really believes that waving his hands around enthusiastically will change water into whisky! But magic usually has a more realistic explanation.

Presto!

Once upon a time…

The new *Tintin* magazine was a hit with Belgian children. Not only did they get the chance to catch up on the latest Tintin adventure every week, but the magazine also published comic strips by other authors. Fun weekly columns included "Interviews with Captain Haddock" (all about boats and the sea), "Major Wings says" (about aeroplanes) and "Tips and tricks" (experiments and practical fun with Professor Calculus). In the third issue of *Tintin* magazine (10 October 1946) kids read about a ghostly magic trick – the "talking head" (see above). How do you think Tintin does this trick? Find out the answer on page 23!

Madame Yamilah the clairvoyant

Furious with his glass of water, Captain Haddock takes Tintin to the music hall to watch Bruno the magician turn water into whisky one more time. But before the magician's show a gentle-looking woman in a pink sari walks on stage. She is put into a trance by a hypnotist...

Once upon a time...

The word "clairvoyance" means the ability to know things beyond the use of the five senses of seeing, hearing, smelling, tasting and touching – "extra-sensory" perception.

Portrait of Hergé by Jacques Van Melkebeke. Note Hergé's Tintin sketch!

Once or twice Hergé asked clairvoyants for advice. One of them, Bertha Jagenau, told Hergé to be careful driving; a few weeks later someone crashed their car into Hergé's. Another time Bertha was at Hergé's house and a portrait of Hergé, painted by his friend Jacques Van Melkebeke, suddenly fell off the wall. The clairvoyant thought this a sign that the painter was a bad influence on Hergé! Some time later Hergé discovered pins sticking in the picture; he never found out who did it. To be on the safe side, the portrait was then put in a cupboard!

Perhaps the most astonishing thing of all is that Hergé himself claimed to have had a clairvoyant experience when his grandfather died. He noted it down on a piece of paper (see above). In English his words read:

"Death of my maternal grandfather (Dufour)
On the evening when he passed away I saw, I am absolutely certain that I saw, a skull on a window frame!... My parents never believed me..."

Spooky! Does a scary face at the window remind you of anyone?

Professor Tarragon's villa

In the days that follow Tintin and Haddock's strange experience at the music hall, one by one the members of the Sanders-Hardiman expedition are struck down by a terrifying mystery illness. The last member to remain unaffected is Professor Hercules Tarragon, who happens to be an old friend of Professor Calculus. Tintin, Haddock, Calculus and Snowy pay Professor Tarragon a visit at his imposing villa.

Once upon a time...

When he wrote this story Hergé was living in a house on Delleur Avenue in Brussels. The house at number 17 on the same street was the perfect model for Tarragon's villa. One day Hergé and his assistant Jacobs went there with sketch-pads. Nobody was in so they spent an hour walking around the house drawing it from different angles. Just as they left they saw a car full of Nazi soldiers pull into the driveway. This was during the war and the house was being used by the Gestapo! Hergé and Jacobs were lucky because if the soldiers had caught them sketching the building it would have seemed very suspicious!

Now let's **Explore and Discover!**

EXPLORE AND DISCOVER

Tintin, Haddock, Calculus and Snowy have been invited to stay the night in Professor Tarragon's creepy villa. As a heavy storm brews outside, Tintin reads a translation of some words that were carved into the walls of an Inca tomb hundreds of years earlier. The strange document makes an eerily accurate prediction...

"After many moons will come seven strangers with pale faces; they will profane the sacred dwellings of he-who-unleashes-the-fire-of-heaven. These vandals will carry the body of the Inca to their own far country. But the curse of the gods will be as their shadow and pursue them over land and sea..."

PREDICTIONS

Predictions are statements that tell of future events before they have happened. Here are some historical predictions:

★ In around 700 B.C., the Jewish prophet Micah said that the Messiah (saviour) would be born in Bethlehem. Hundreds of years later, Jesus Christ was born in the small town!

★ In the year 1555, Frenchman Nostradamus published a book of predictions, including one which mentioned London and the "ancient lady" being "burned by fire in the year '66". In 1666 the Great Fire of London destroyed most of the medieval parts of the city.

★ Hundreds of years ago, the Italian artist and inventor Leonardo da Vinci (1452-1519) drafted diagrams, including submarines, parachutes, helicopters, aeroplanes and steam engines! But his knowledge of engineering and skill at drawing make these predictions more scientific than supernatural.

Although the crystal balls in this story are used for poisonous purposes, traditionally a crystal ball can be used by a clairvoyant to help them know things or predict the future. Apparently Nostradamus used one, although how much it helped him is not clear. For example, he did say that a "great king of terror" would "come from the sky" in 1999. One or two people panicked but nothing happened, showing that sometimes predictions come true and sometimes they don't!

Leonardo da Vinci, self portrait, 1470s.

Nostradamus, by Aime de Lemud, 1840.

THE FIRE OF HEAVEN

Tintin is reading about "He-who-unleashes-the-fire-of-heaven" when suddenly a bolt of lightning strikes the chimney of Professor Tarragon's villa. A fiery ball shoots out of the fireplace, racing around the room and wreaking havoc! It shreds Tarragon's clothes and lifts Calculus onto a table. And then – "BANG!" – the fireball explodes! Good gracious! The mummy has been vaporised! But Rascar Capac will be back later that night…

BALL LIGHTNING

Ball lightning is a rare atmospheric phenomenon where a glowing ball, lasting for a few seconds, appears during a thunderstorm. Sometimes the ball explodes! Scientists have proposed that ball lightning is microwave radiation, vaporised silicon or even tiny black holes (points of extremely strong gravity in space). But ball lightning still has not fully been explained.

★ As well as ball lightning seen on the ground and inside buildings, there have been accounts of ball lightning appearing in aeroplanes and submarines.

★ Tsar Nicholas II of Russia (1868-1918) said that when he was a child, he once saw ball lightning whirling around a church.

★ A British magazine reported that in 1809 three "balls of fire" struck a ship named the HMS *Warren Hastings*, setting the mast on fire and killing two men.

★ In 1638 there was a great storm in Britain. Ball lightning struck and entered a church in a town called Widecombe-in-the-Moor, damaging walls, smashing benches and breaking windows. Later some people blamed two of the congregation for playing cards during the sermon, saying they had made God angry!

RASCAR CAPAC

Rascar Capac is the most scary character in *The Adventures of Tintin* – it's official!

When you put together a mummy (real – read about them on the next page), a spooky prediction (real – even if some of them don't come true), ball lightning (real – but no-one knows exactly what it is) and nightmares (real – we've all had them!) then you're bound to get absolute terror!

Hergé was so pleased with his new character that he drew a large picture of the petrifying Peruvian mummy for the title page of the first edition of *The Seven Crystal Balls* (see above). But Casterman, the publisher of Tintin, soon wrote to him asking to change this picture, because it was scaring little children too much!

Peruvian mummy from the Royal Museum of Art and History, Brussels.

★ A mummy is a dead body that has been preserved and does not decay.

★ The preservation process may have happened naturally through unusual conditions such as cold or lack of air, or intentionally (for religious or cultural reasons) through the removal of bodily organs and the use of various chemicals.

★ The most famous mummies come from Egypt, but the Ancient Egyptians didn't just mummify human beings – over a million animal mummies have been discovered in the country. Watch out Snowy!

Illustration of an Egyptian dog mummy.

REAL CARS

After reading about so many spooky things which we don't want to believe are real but think we might, here are a couple of ordinary cars from the story that are very real!

After Professor Tarragon has fallen victim to the curse of Rascar Capac, Professor Calculus disappears in suspicious circumstances. A black car speeds away! For this car Hergé copied an Opel Olympia. The 1947 model of this car (shown below) had an aerial for the radio.

REAL TOYS

The police have contacted Captain Haddock to tell him that they believe Professor Calculus's kidnappers went to the port of Westermouth. Haddock hops behind the wheel of his yellow Lincoln Zephyr as he gives chase with Tintin and Snowy in the passenger seats!

Check out this scale model of the car – a real collectible that Tintin fans can buy today.

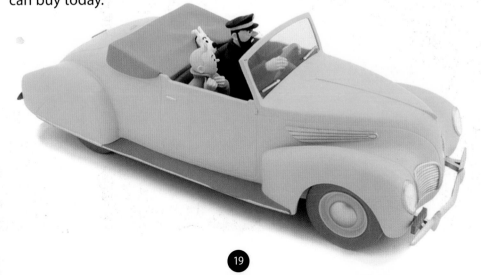

SCALLYWAGS SAVE THE DAY

The trail has gone cold and if it wasn't for the two scallywags the kidnappers would have gotten clean away. Luckily one of the objects they used for their painful prank on Captain Haddock turns out to be Professor Calculus's hat, an important clue to his whereabouts.

QUICK AND FLUPKE

The two naughty boys in the story were not just made up by Hergé for *The Seven Crystal Balls*; they are real comic strip characters with their own series – *Quick and Flupke* (see your Young Readers *Cigars of the Pharaoh*)! Hergé wrote many short stories for the two rapscallions; you can read one of them on the opposite page!

A SIMPLE QUESTION

Excuse me Madam, have you seen our glider?

OFF TO PERU

It turns out that Professor Calculus is on board a ship bound for Peru. There's no time to lose – Tintin and Captain Haddock catch the next available flight to South America!

Hergé copied a Short Sunderland aircraft – check out the photo from his archives. He liked to copy real vehicles precisely, but in this case maybe he used a different image: the round bumps – radar antenna – underneath the wings are missing from his drawing.

SO... REAL OR NOT?

What is real and what is not in this story? You have to decide! But like Tintin, you can find out more in the next adventure, *Prisoners of the Sun*!

TINTIN'S GRAND ADVENTURE

The first Tintin comic strips to be published in *Tintin* magazine were from *The Seven Crystal Balls*. From now on, the rest of the Tintin adventures would be published page by page, week by week, in the magazine, before being sold as books. *Tintin* magazine became very popular and it wasn't long before an issue was launched for France (1948), which was also a spectacular success. Unfortunately for many children around the world, the magazine was never published in English!

Trivia: *The Seven Crystal Balls*

The "talking head" magic trick (see page 7) from Tintin *magazine* is done by placing mirrors in the right positions under the table, to hide the person underneath who is sticking their head up through a hole in the table!

Knife-throwing, shown on page 10 of the adventure, is something real you might see in a circus. But look carefully – an extra knife appears between the frames on strip 3 and strip 4. Ghost knife-thrower or mistake by Hergé?

Today you can buy a Rascar Capac fridge magnet. There is no better way to stop anyone stealing your milk!

Some of the strips published in Tintin *magazine* were later removed when the story came out as a book. One of these strips shows an extra scene at the music hall, where the clairvoyant tells the audience that Captain Haddock's pocket is full of monocles and everyone laughs!

· HERGÉ ·
LES AVENTURES DE TINTIN
LES 7 BOULES DE CRISTAL
CASTERMAN

The original cover for *The Seven Crystal Balls* (1948)